SCIENCE MAKERS

Making with
FORCES

Anna Claybourne

BUILD **AMAZING PROJECTS** WITH **INSPIRATIONAL SCIENTISTS,** **ARTISTS** AND **ENGINEERS**

First published in Great Britain in 2018 by Wayland
Copyright © Hodder and Stoughton, 2018
All rights reserved.

Editor: Sarah Silver
Designer: Eoin Norton
Picture researcher: Diana Morris

ISBN 978 1 5263 0542 8

All photographs by Eoin Norton for Wayland except the following:
BPK Berlin/Wikimedia Commons: 10tl. Chemical Heritage Foundation. Photo by Will Brown/CC
Wikimedia Commons: 14t. Steve Collender/Shutterstock: 17tr. Jeffrey Coolidge/Getty Images:
26t, 29b. Corbis via Getty Images: 26b. © Lin Emery/DACS, London/VAGA, NY 2017: 25br. The
Evening Standard/Hulton Archive/Getty Images: 18tr. Pat Falconer/REX /Shutterstock: 7bc.
Haags Historisch Museum/Wikimedia Commons: 8tl. Ina van Hateren/Shutterstock: 5t. Herbert/
AP/Rex/Shutterstock: 24bl. Jan Hindstroem/Shutterstock: 4b. Franz Hubmann/Imagno/
Topfoto: 22tl. Jam World Images/Alamy: 23b © Theo Jansen/DACS, London 2017: 5b. Aleksandr
Kurganov/Shutterstock: 19b. Leemage/UIG/Getty Images: 6tl. illustration from Renitenza
Certissima dell' Aqua alla Compressione, R Maggiotti, 1648: 12c. NMM Greenwich/Wikimedia
Commons: 6tr. Pupes/Shutterstock: 4t. Sashkin/Shutterstock: 9b. TU- Braunschweig/
Wikimedia Commons: 20t. Paul Velgos/Shutterstock: 17br. CC Wikimedia Commons: 10tr, 18tl.

Every attempt has been made to clear copyright. Should there be any
inadvertent omission please apply to the publisher for rectification.

Printed in China

Wayland, an imprint of
Hachette Children's Group
Part of Hodder and Stoughton
Carmelite House
50 Victoria Embankment
London EC4Y 0DZ

An Hachette UK Company
www.hachette.co.uk
www.hachettechildrens.co.uk

Note:
In preparation of this book, all due care has been exercised with regard to the instructions, activities
and techniques depicted. The publishers regret that they can accept no liability for any loss or injury
sustained. Always follow manufacturers' advice when using electric and battery-powered appliances.

The website addresses (URLs) included in this book were valid at the time of going to press.
However, because of the nature of the Internet, it is possible that some addresses may have
changed, or sites may have changed or closed down since publication. While the author
and publishers regret any inconvenience this may cause to the readers, no responsibility
for any such changes can be accepted by either the author or the publishers.

CONTENTS

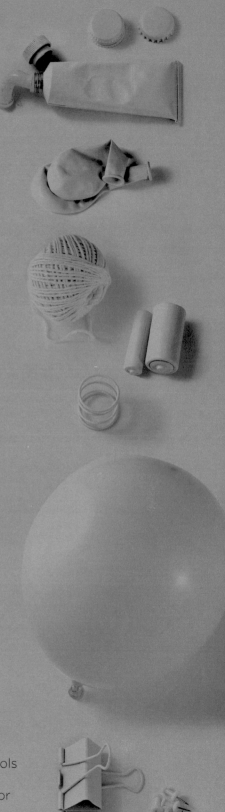

TAKE CARE!

These projects can be made with everyday objects, materials and tools that you can find at home, or in a supermarket, hobby store or DIY store. However, some do involve working with things that are sharp or breakable, or need extra strength to operate. Make sure you have an adult on hand to supervise and to help with anything that could be dangerous, and get permission before you try out any of the projects.

UNDERSTANDING FORCES

In science lessons, forces are often described as 'pushes and pulls'. It sounds simple, but that's about all there is to it! Forces make all kinds of movements and actions happen, and they're all around us, all the time. For example, when you pick up a heavy bag, your hand pulls it upwards, while gravity pulls it downwards. A row of dominoes topple down because the force of each one falling pushes the next one – and so on.

TYPES OF FORCES

Although all forces push or pull, they can do this in lots of ways, and there are many different types of forces. They include:

 Applied force – a direct push or pull on an object

 Friction – a force that slows or stops objects when they rub together

 Upthrust – the force that makes something float as the fluid it is in pushes upwards

 Gravity – a force that pulls objects towards each other, even if they're not touching

 Electric force – a force produced by objects being electrically charged

 Air resistance – a slowing force that happens when an object moves through air

Throwing an object involves several forces working at once.

MANY FORCES

Forces are always working in all kinds of ways, not just one at a time. In this picture you can see several forces in action.

1. **Pushing force of your arm**

2. **Pulling force of gravity**

3. **Slowing force of air resistance**

4. **Friction force when the object hits the ground**

FORCE INVENTIONS

Without forces, nothing would move at all. So forces are often an important part of human inventions. Since ancient times we've been coming up with machines, tools and gadgets to help us use forces to do jobs more easily. Think of boats, bows and arrows, food mixers, spin dryers, or industrial robots. And of course, one of the greatest inventions of all time – the wheel, which makes it much easier to move things around.

A water wheel uses the force of falling water to create a turning force.

Dutch scientist and artist Theo Jansen (1948–) builds huge sculptures known as 'strandbeests' that 'walk' like animals when blown by the wind.

FORCES IN ART

Traditionally, most artworks have stayed still, once they were finished. It took a good understanding of forces to make a large sculpture, but the art itself didn't usually display forces in action. In the last century, though, more and more art has been made that uses forces to work. There are huge outdoor artworks that move when pushed by wind or water, and sculptures with moving parts that create a sequence of motions. Some artists also use natural forces to help them make images.

SPEEDING CAR
STUNT RAMP

Copy Galileo, one of the greatest scientists of all time, by rolling cars down a ramp!

MAKER PROFILE:

Galileo Galilei
(1564–1642)

Galileo Galilei was a great Italian scientist. He was always experimenting, testing and making. One of his many obsessions was rolling balls and other objects down slopes. He figured out how objects accelerate, or speed up, as they fall or roll downhill. He realised that they don't just speed up a bit – they keep on getting faster and faster.

A 17th century painting showing Galileo demonstrating his discovery.

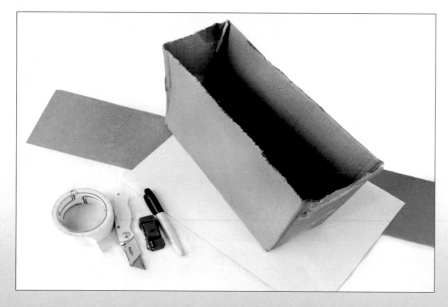

WHAT YOU NEED

- cardboard box
- marker pen
- craft knife or scissors
- large sheets of strong, flexible card
- packing tape or duct tape
- long piece of stiff card from a large cardboard box
- a toy car

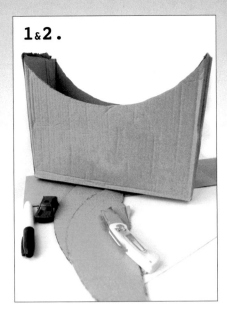

1 & 2.

Step 1.
Draw a curved line on the side of the cardboard box. With adult help, cut along the curve and cut off the rest of the side of the box.

Step 2.
Use the piece you have cut off as a template to draw the same curve on the other side of the box. Cut along the curve and cut off the ends of the box so you have a curved shape at the top of the box.

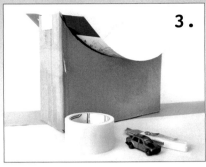

3.

Step 3.
Take a large piece of card and cut a piece to fit along the curve. Gently bend the card and tape it to the box.

4.

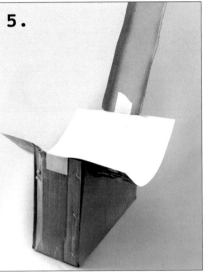

5.

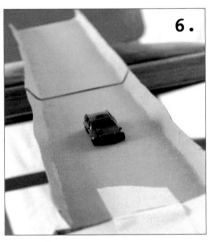

6.

Step 4.
To make a speed ramp, use a piece of stiff card 1-2 m long (it can be two pieces joined together) and 10-12 cm wide. Fold the edges up to make walls along the ramp about 2 cm high.

Step 5.
Rest one end of the long ramp on a windowsill, table or chair, using tape to hold it in place. Line the other end up with the curved ramp, and tape them together to make a smooth join.

Step 6.
Try rolling toy cars down the ramp, first from low down, then from higher up. How fast do they go? How high do they have to start from to make them go fast enough to fly off the ramp?

PICKING UP SPEED

As Galileo found, the further an object rolls, the faster it goes. Cars rolled from higher up the ramp should pick up enough speed to fly off the ramp. The cars roll downwards because they are pulled towards the ground by gravity. As gravity keeps pulling on them, even when they are moving, it keeps adding to their speed.

BEAT DE CREED!

Stunt drivers really do make car jumps like this in real life. Top stuntwoman Jacquie de Creed beat the distance record in 1983 with an amazing 71 metre jump. That's like jumping 18 cars lined up end-to-end. If you have enough toy cars, line them up between the ramps and see if you can beat that!

Try making a landing ramp too, and see if you can make a car jump the gap and land safely.

NEWTON'S CRADLE

Newton's cradle, a famous science toy, is easy to make and fascinating to watch.

MAKER PROFILE:

Christiaan Huygens
(c. 1629–1695)

Christiaan Huygens, a Dutch scientist, is mainly known for his work on space. He was also inspired by another scientist, Sir Isaac Newton, and his ideas about forces and movement. Using these ideas, Huygens built a device with swinging balls that crashed into each other, to demonstrate how motion can be passed on from one object to another. Today, the invention is still a popular toy.

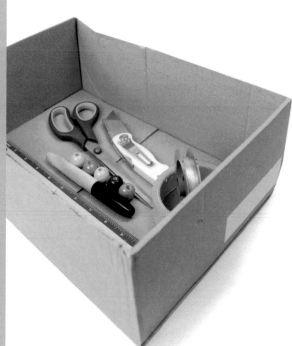

WHAT YOU NEED

- a small, strong cardboard box without a lid
- strong scissors or craft knife
- ruler
- marker pen
- at least 2 m of beading thread or fine string
- five large, heavy, round beads made of plastic, wood or metal (not glass), with large holes
- sticky tape

1.

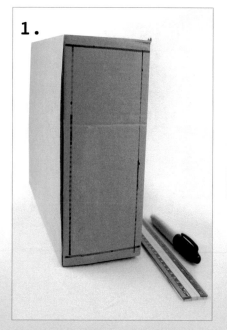

2.

Step 1.
Use the ruler and marker pen to draw a frame on each side of the box, about 1 cm in from the edge all round.

Step 2.
With an adult to help, carefully cut along the lines with a craft knife or scissors, to remove a large rectangle from each side of the box. You will be left with a simple frame.

3.

Step 3.
Cut five pieces of thread, each about 40 cm long. Take one piece, thread it through a bead, then thread it around and through again, so that the bead is held in the middle of the thread. Repeat this for the rest of the beads and thread.

4.

Step 4.
Now tie the threads to the sides of the frame, so that the beads hang down in the middle. Use loose knots that can be adjusted easily. When all five beads are in place, adjust the threads so that the beads are all touching in a row.

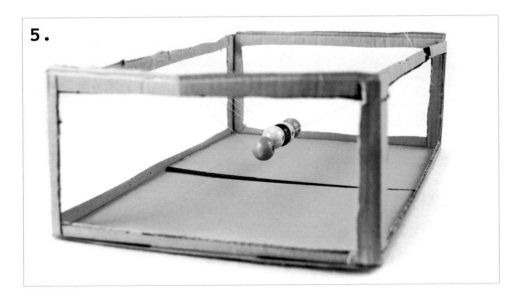

5.

Step 5.
Once the beads are neatly lined up, tie the knots tightly, or use sticky tape to hold them in place. Trim off any surplus thread. Test the cradle by pulling a bead at one end away from the others, then letting it drop back towards them.

PASSING IT ON

If it works, you should see the first bead stop when it hits the next one, and the bead at the other end move away instead. The three beads in the middle stay where they are. This is because the energy from the first bead passes through them all, until it passes into the last one, which is free to move. It may look strange, but it follows a law of science discovered by Newton, know as conservation of momentum. It means that the movement energy does not disappear, even if it is not in the same object that it started in. It can pass from one object to another.

MAKING FLIGHT HISTORY

The Montgolfier brothers used paper to make their first hot air balloons – you can do the same.

An engraving showing the first human flight, on 21 November 1783.

MAKER PROFILE:

Joseph-Michel Montgolfier
(1740–1810)

Jacques-Étienne Montgolfier
(1745–1799)

Joseph and Étienne Montgolfier were brothers whose family ran a paper-making business. They began working on hot air balloons after Joseph saw how smoke from a fire made cloth rise upwards. The brothers built bigger and bigger boxes and bags, using paper and cloth. Filling them with smoke from fires made them rise into the air. By September 1783, they were building balloons big enough to lift animals. And in November 1783, the first ever flight with humans on board took off in Paris.

WHAT YOU NEED

- four large sheets of tissue paper
- marker pen
- scissors
- glue stick or PVA glue
- thin card
- hairdryer

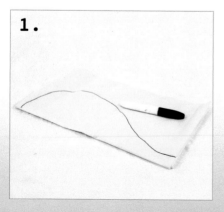

1.

Step 1.
Open out your tissue paper and put the sheets in a pile, neatly on top of each other. Fold the whole pile in half, and use the marker pen to draw one half of a long, narrow balloon shape.

Step 2.
Holding all the paper together at the folded side, cut along the line to make four balloon shapes. Separate the shapes and fold them in half again.

2.

3.

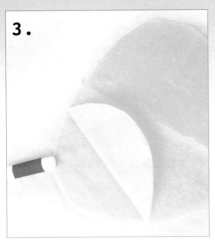

Step 3.
Carefully put a thin layer of glue around the edge of one half of the first piece of paper, and lie another folded piece on top, so that the two edges stick together.

4.

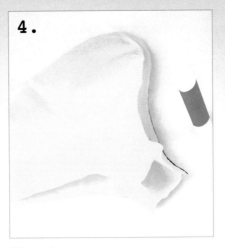

Step 4.
Repeat with the next three pieces. Finally, fold the two remaining cut edges back and glue them together as well. Glue adds weight, so try not to use too much.

5.

Step 5.
Glue any gaps at the top of your balloon shut. Cut a strip of card about 2-3 cm wide, and glue it around the opening at the bottom of the balloon, in a ring shape.

6.

Step 6.
Once the glue is dry, hold the balloon up, keeping it flat. Ask an adult to switch on the hairdryer on a low setting, and use the hot air to fill the balloon (this will happen quite quickly). Once it's full of hot air, let go!

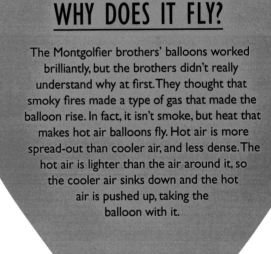

WHY DOES IT FLY?

The Montgolfier brothers' balloons worked brilliantly, but the brothers didn't really understand why at first. They thought that smoky fires made a type of gas that made the balloon rise. In fact, it isn't smoke, but heat that makes hot air balloons fly. Hot air is more spread-out than cooler air, and less dense. The hot air is lighter than the air around it, so the cooler air sinks down and the hot air is pushed up, taking the balloon with it.

If it doesn't work very well, this could be because you're already in a warm room. It might work better somewhere cooler.

PRESSURE DIVER

Make a diving octopus that sinks and floats with the squeeze of a bottle.

MAKER PROFILE:

Raffaelo Magiotti
(1597–1656)

Magiotti is known for designing a device now called the Cartesian diver (or, as it used to be known, the Cartesian devil). He made it to demonstrate that while air can easily be compressed or squashed into a smaller space, it's much harder to do this with water. His creation is still used as a toy and science experiment to this day.

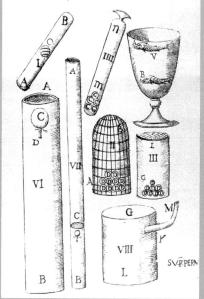

My invention isn't about cold or heat, but about the resistance to compression.
– Raffaelo Magiotti

An illustration from Magiotti's book, *Water's Resistance to Compression*, showing different designs for the Cartesian diver.

WHAT YOU NEED

- rubber glove
- scissors
- squeezy plastic medicine dropper
- sticky tack
- permanent marker
- waterproof tape or duct tape
- large clear plastic drinks bottle, with a lid
- large bowl
- water

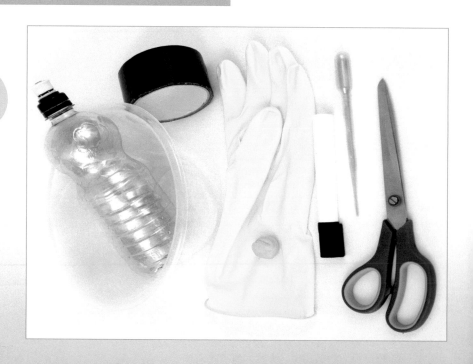

1.

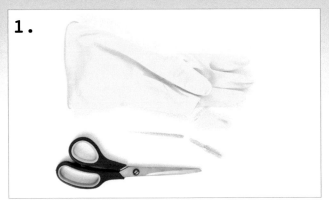

Step 1.
Cut most of the long tube off the plastic dropper, leaving a short stalk. Take the rubber glove and cut off the smallest finger.

2.

Step 2.
Cut off the very tip of the finger to leave a small hole, and cut the lower end of the glove finger into octopus legs. Press a ring of sticky tack around the lower end of the dropper to make it heavier.

3.

Step 3.
Stretch the cut glove over the dropper and tape it in place with a small piece of strong tape. Add eyes using the marker pen.

4.

Step 4.
Fill your bottle with water right to the brim. Fill the bowl with water too. You now need to put some water inside your octopus, so that it just floats.

5.

Step 5.
Squeeze the dropper and use it to suck up some water, leaving some air inside. Put it in the bowl. If it sinks, squeeze a little water out. It needs to just float, so that most of it hangs down below the water surface.

6.

Step 6.
When your octopus is ready, push it into the bottle of water, top up the water to the brim, and put the lid on tightly. Squeeze the bottle with both hands to make the octopus dive. Let go to make it float again.

UP AND DOWN

What's going on? The octopus floats at first because its overall density – how much it weighs for its size – is less than that of water. When you squeeze the bottle, you squeeze the water inside too. Water doesn't 'squash' easily – it's very hard to compress it into a smaller space. As the bottle is full, the only place for the water to go is into the diver. The diver has an air bubble inside, and air is easy to squash. The water pushing in squeezes the air, and it gets smaller. Now, the diver contains more water, so its overall density is greater, and it sinks. When you let go, the squeezed air pushes some of the water back out, and it floats up again.

ROCKET POWER

Use the 'springiness' of the air, discovered by Robert Boyle, to fire rockets.

MAKER PROFILE:

Robert Boyle
(1627–1691)

Irish-born Robert Boyle was a brilliant all-round scientist. He studied and experimented in many areas, including chemicals, forces, sound, light, freezing and air pressure.

He was especially interested in how air could be compressed and squeezed. He made a J-shaped tube with a pocket of air in the end, and used mercury (a heavy liquid metal) to push on the air. He found that the more you squeeze air and put it under pressure, the more it pushes back, just like a bouncy spring.

There is a Spring, or Elastical power in the Air we live in.
– Robert Boyle

SQUEEZING THE AIR

These pictures show how Boyle's tube worked. The curved end was sealed, and the tube contained some mercury, trapping a little air at the sealed end. Boyle added more mercury to see what would happen.

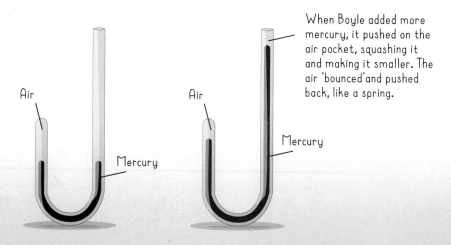

Air

Mercury

Air

Mercury

When Boyle added more mercury, it pushed on the air pocket, squashing it and making it smaller. The air 'bounced' and pushed back, like a spring.

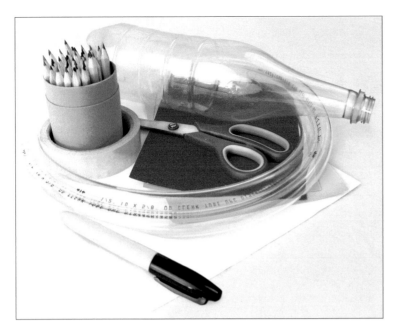

WHAT YOU NEED

- paper and card
- a piece of plastic tubing, around 1 m long and 2 cm wide
- marker pen
- scissors
- colouring pens or pencils
- a large plastic fizzy drinks bottle
- strong sticky tape or duct tape
- a computer and printer (optional)

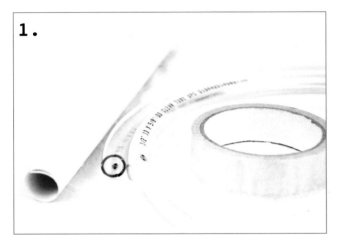

Step 1.

Take a piece of paper and roll it around the end of the plastic tubing, to make a rocket body that's just slightly wider than the plastic tubing. Fix the paper rocket with sticky tape.

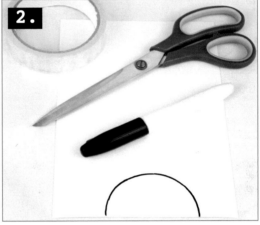

Step 2.

Draw around a round object (such as a roll of tape) onto more paper to make a half circle shape.

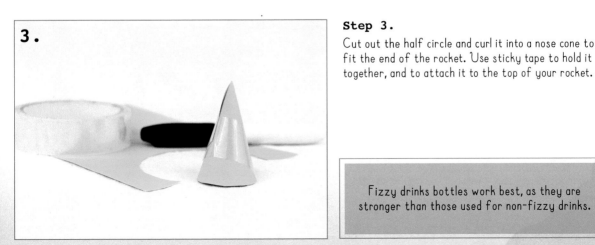

Step 3.

Cut out the half circle and curl it into a nose cone to fit the end of the rocket. Use sticky tape to hold it together, and to attach it to the top of your rocket.

Fizzy drinks bottles work best, as they are stronger than those used for non-fizzy drinks.

4.

Step 4.

Cut three or four triangles or curved fin shapes from card, and use sticky tape to fix them onto the sides of the rocket near the bottom. Draw on windows and decorations too if you like.

5.

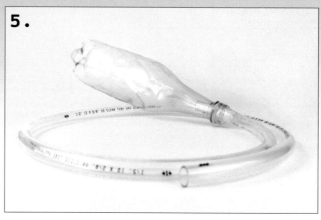

Step 5.

Take the lid off the bottle, if there is one. Insert the plastic tubing into the top of the bottle, if possible. If the tubing does not fit inside the bottle, line up the bottle opening and the tube and use strong sticky tape to join them together.

6.

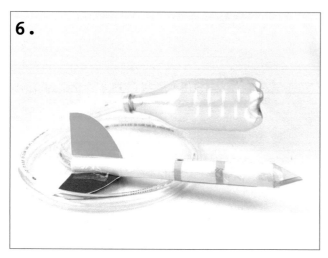

TAKE CARE!

If it works, the rocket will go FAST. Don't aim it at other people, animals, or anything breakable! If possible, test it in a big room, or outdoors if you can, and see how far it will go.

Step 6.

You can now test your rocket. Put the bottle on the floor, and fit the rocket onto the other end of the tube. Aim the rocket, and fire it by stamping hard on the bottle.

7.

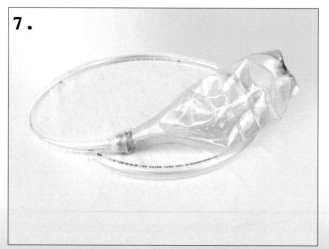

Step 7.

To re-use the shooter, blow into the tube to re-inflate the bottle.

8.

Step 8.

Draw a selection of targets, such as planets, moons or spacecraft, onto circles of paper (or print out pictures from the Internet). Give each target a score number, and stick them to a wall or a large cardboard box. Take turns shooting at the targets and keep score. Each player could make and decorate their own rocket to use.

AIR PRESSURE POWER

When you stamp on the bottle, you suddenly squash the air inside, putting it under much greater pressure. The molecules it is made of are forced closer to each other. Because of this, the air pushes hard against the container it is in. It can't escape from the bottle, so it zooms down the tube and forces the rocket off the end at high speed.

Imagine if the bottle had water in it, which is much harder to squash. You wouldn't be able to stamp it flat quickly – it would only go down slowly, and the water would come out of the tube slowly too. It's the sudden squeezing of the air that puts it under pressure, and makes it suddenly push outwards again.

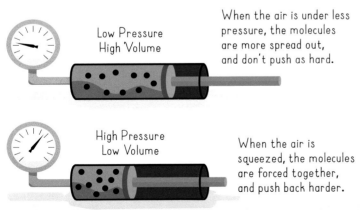

Low Pressure
High Volume

When the air is under less pressure, the molecules are more spread out, and don't push as hard.

High Pressure
Low Volume

When the air is squeezed, the molecules are forced together, and push back harder.

INFLATABLE SCIENCE

You can feel the effect of air's 'spring' when you blow up a balloon, airbed or bouncy castle. As you force more and more air into the space inside, you are squashing it and putting it under pressure. When you press down or bounce on it, you can feel the air inside pushing back.

FLOATING ON AIR

Make an easy model hovercraft that works like the real thing!

MAKER PROFILE:

Sir Christopher Cockerell
(1910–1999)

British engineer and boat-builder Christopher Cockerell is famous for inventing the hovercraft in the early 1950s. People had already thought of blowing air underneath a boat to reduce drag. But it was hard to get enough air in, and to stop it from escaping too fast.

Cockerell built a model using a coffee tin, a cat food tin and an air blower. Instead of just filling a space under the vehicle, the moving air flowed through a narrow gap around the sides, making it push down much harder. From this idea, he developed a full-sized hovercraft.

Cockerell's hovercraft SRN1 on the River Thames in London, UK, 1959.

People think there aren't more inventions to invent, but there are.
– Christopher Cockerell

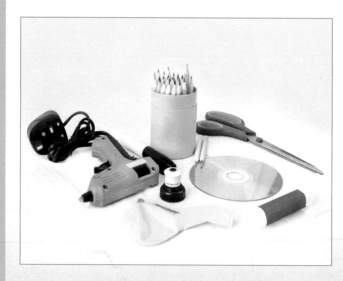

WHAT YOU NEED

- an old, unwanted CD (if you don't have any, try a charity shop)
- paper
- scissors
- colouring pens or pencils
- glue stick
- spout-shaped lid from a water bottle
- strong glue or a hot glue gun
- a balloon

1.

Step 1.
Draw around the CD onto a piece of paper, including the hole in the middle. Cut out the circle and the hole, and draw a design on the paper.

2.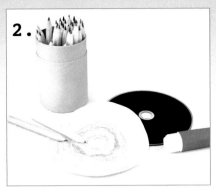

Step 2.
Use the glue stick to attach your design onto the CD, making sure it is well-glued all around the middle. Leave it to dry completely.

3.

Step 3.
With an adult to help, use strong glue or a hot glue gun to glue the spout over the central hole in the CD, making sure it is well glued all around. Leave to dry.

4.

Step 4.
Blow up the balloon, and twist the opening around a few times to hold the air in. Stretch the opening over the bottle spout, and put the hovercraft on a smooth, hard floor or table.

5.

Step 5.
To start the hovercraft, untwist the balloon so that the air can flow out. Give the hovercraft a gentle push, and see how far it goes!

MIND THE GAP!

Try to push your CD along without the balloon and it will soon stop, thanks to friction with the ground. Friction is a dragging, gripping force that happens when materials rub together. It's the same with a boat on water – friction between the hull and the water creates drag, slowing the boat down.

A hovercraft reduces drag by blowing a layer of flowing air between the surfaces. As air is made of gas, it contains fewer molecules than solids or liquids, and there is less drag.

Cockerell's hovercraft directed air along narrow channels to make it blow harder, and lift the hovercraft higher. In the CD version, the air blows through the narrow hole in the middle, pushing the CD off the ground in a similar way.

Hovercraft, like this rescue hovercraft, are amphibious – they can travel over both land and water.

WHALE RACE

MAKER PROFILE:

Agnes Pockels
(1862–1935)

German experimenter Agnes Pockels wanted to study science, but at the time, most universities weren't open to women. However, her brother did go to university, so she borrowed his books and did her own experiments on water and surface tension. Surface tension is a force that makes water molecules pull towards each other, making a 'skin' on the water surface that can hold up small objects. To help her experiments, Pockels invented the Pockels trough, a tray-like device for measuring surface tension.

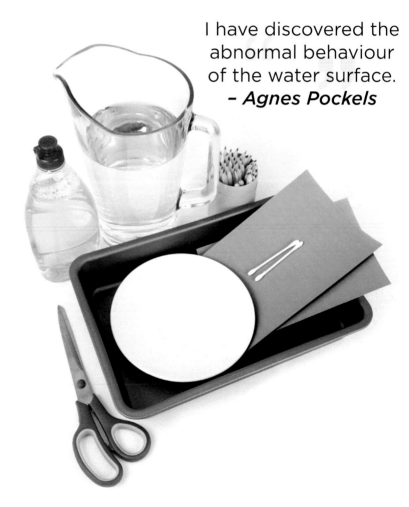

I have discovered the abnormal behaviour of the water surface.
– Agnes Pockels

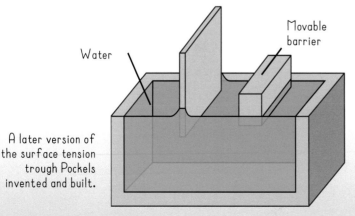

Water

Movable barrier

A later version of the surface tension trough Pockels invented and built.

WHAT YOU NEED

- a large, shallow tray, such as a baking tray
- a jug of water
- thin card
- colouring pens or pencils
- scissors
- washing-up liquid
- a saucer
- cotton buds

Step 1.
Put the tray on a solid, flat surface and use the jug to carefully fill it with water. Wait for the water to settle down and become still.

Step 2.
On a piece of card, draw or trace a whale shape like this, with a notch in the middle of its tail. Carefully cut it out, keeping it as flat as possible.

Step 3.
Make a whale for each person who wants to race. You can colour them in, add eyes, and number them too, so you can tell whose is whose.

Step 4.
Put some washing-up liquid on the saucer and have the cotton buds ready. (If you don't have any cotton buds, you can use the blunt ends of pencils.)

Step 5.
Put the whales in the water at one end of the tray. To start the race, each person dips their cotton bud in the washing-up liquid, and touches it to the notch on the back of their whale. Now watch your whales race!

SURFACE MOTION

Surface tension works because water molecules have a force that pulls them towards each other. Inside the water, they are pulled in all directions, but at the surface, they are only pulled inwards and sideways, making a kind of barrier. This is what causes the skin-like surface that can hold up small objects such as pins.

Adding a detergent, such as washing-up liquid, to the water reduces surface tension behind the whale. This is because the water molecules there are now attracted to the detergent, and less to each other. But the surface tension in front of the whale is still strong, so the water surface there quickly pulls away from the detergent – taking the whale with it.

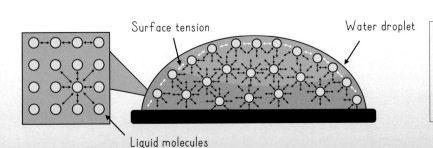

Surface tension

Water droplet

Liquid molecules

TIP!
If the whales start to get soggy, leave them to dry out, or just make some more.

PENDULUM ART

Get science to help you create amazing art, using a pendulum.

MAKER PROFILE:

Max Ernst
(1891–1976)

German painter, sculptor and writer Max Ernst loved experimenting with new ways of making art. One of the many things he tried was swinging a paint can with a hole in it – a type of pendulum – to and fro to make swirls and loops of paint. He called this method 'oscillation'. Ernst would then add colours and other elements to the picture.

WHAT YOU NEED

- a door frame
- lots of newspaper
- sticky tape
- an empty squeezy bottle with a lid, such as a washing-up liquid bottle
- strong scissors
- hole punch
- string
- drawing pin

- water-based paint (either premixed or powder paint) in different colours
- plastic container
- spoon
- large pieces of plain paper

TAKE CARE:
If you don't have a hole punch, ask an adult to make the holes with scissors.

Step 1.
First, spread a thick layer of newspaper all over the floor, under and up the sides of the door frame, attaching it with sticky tape.

Step 2.
Make sure your squeezy bottle and lid are clean. With an adult to help, cut off the base of the bottle. Use a hole punch to make two holes in the bottle, near where the base has been cut off.

2.

3.

Step 3.

Cut a piece of string about 2.5 m long, thread it through the holes in the bottle, and tie the end so that the bottle can hang up.

4.

Step 4.

Ask an adult to fix the other end of the string to the door frame, using the drawing pin, so that the bottle hangs upside-down about 10-20 cm off the ground.

5.

Step 5.

Put plenty of paint in the plastic container, and add water bit by bit, mixing until you have a thick but runny liquid paint.

6.

Step 6.

Making sure the lid is closed, carefully pour the paint into the squeezy bottle. With clean, dry hands, spread out a large piece of paper under the bottle.

7.

Step 7.

Pull the bottle slightly to one side, open the lid, and then let the bottle swing over the paper, giving it a slight push to the side so that it moves in a circle or oval, dripping paint as it goes.

8.

Step 8.

When you're happy with the painting, stop the bottle and close the lid. If you like you can try adding more colours. As the paint is quite watery, it will take several hours to dry.

SWINGING SCIENCE

A pendulum swings because the force of gravity pulls it downwards, while momentum keeps it moving. The way the Earth spins also affects it. Gradually, air resistance slows the pendulum down, and this also changes the pattern.

A giant pendulum in a museum in Valencia, Spain. The balls are knocked down as the rotation of the Earth makes the pendulum move in different directions.

KINETIC CREATIONS

Build a sculpture that moves and spins in the slightest breeze.

WHAT YOU NEED

- a tall glass bottle
- a cork that fits in the bottle
- sewing pins
- small beads
- drinking straws
- polystyrene craft balls in different sizes
- glue
- scissors
- lightweight materials, such as card, aluminium foil, corks and feathers

MAKER PROFILE:

Lin Emery
(1928–)

American artist Lin Emery is a leading kinetic sculptor. She makes delicately balanced 3D works of art that are powered by water, or move in the wind, twirling and spinning around yet always staying in balance.

1&2.

Step 1.
Stand your bottle on a flat, firm surface and push the cork into the top, so that it's sticking out. This is the base for your sculpture.

Step 2.
Carefully push a pin right through the middle of one of the straws. Thread two or three beads onto the pin below the straw, then push the pin into the middle of the cork. Make sure that the straw can spin around freely.

3.

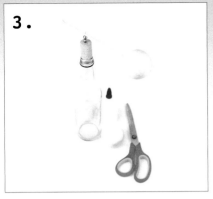

Step 3.
Ask an adult to help you use the scissors to make a small hole in a polystyrene ball. Put a drop of glue in the hole, then push it onto one end of the straw you have already added to the bottle. Do the same on the other end too.

4.

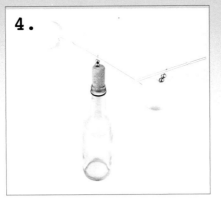

Step 4.
Push a pin through a new straw, thread some beads onto the pin, and push the pin into the polystyrene ball. The new straw should also spin around. Add a new straw to the polystyrene ball on the other end in the same way.

5.

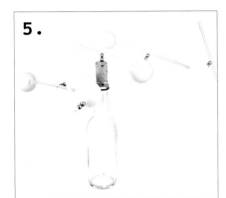

Step 5.
Keep adding more straws in the same way, until you have several branches that can turn and move. Try experimenting with different lengths of straw, and with putting the pins in different positions. Spin them as you add them to check different parts do not crash into each other.

6.

Step 6.
You can now add interesting shapes or objects to the moving ends of the straws, such as pieces cut out of cardboard or foil. Try different sizes and weights to make the sculpture balance evenly.

Here are some ideas for shapes and patterns.

IN THE BALANCE

A sculpture like this will stay balanced as long as there's an equal amount of weight on each side of the central pin, and each moving arm of the sculpture is also balanced on its own pin in the same way. Emery builds her sculptures so that even when all the parts are moving, the balance stays equal. This can take some time to get right! When it works, the sculpture will move gently in a breeze, or when you blow it.

Lin Emery's stainless steel sculpture, *Deva* (1986), can be seen at Marina Bay in Singapore.

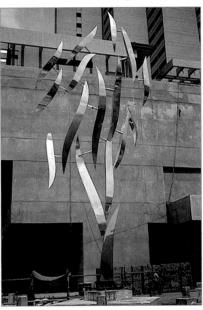

The elements are derived from nature, and I borrow natural elements — wind, water, magnets — to set them in motion.
– Lin Emery

FOLLOW THE FORCE!

A Rube Goldberg machine combines many forces in a sequence, just to do one simple job!

This Rube Goldberg machine has lots of stages and parts for the simple task of turning on a light.

MAKER PROFILE:

Rube Goldberg
(1883–1970)

Rube Goldberg was an American cartoonist, engineer and sculptor. He was famous for drawing – and sometimes building – hilarious, complicated 'Rube Goldberg machines'. They used a chain reaction of comedy movements to do one simple task – like pouring a cup of tea, or ringing a bell.

Today, Rube Goldberg machines are more popular than ever. They are used in advertisements, games and pop videos, and there are competitions to build the best designs.

The machines are a symbol of man's capacity for exerting maximum effort to achieve minimal results.
- *Rube Goldberg*

WHAT YOU NEED

A Rube Goldberg machine can be built using all kinds of everyday objects. This list includes some of the most common and useful items people use, but you can add others, as long as they're not breakable or dangerous. Avoid anything sharp, hot, fragile or messy, and check with an adult before taking things to use. For our Rube Goldberg machine we used the following items:

- balloon
- a cardboard tube
- paper cups
- a toy car
- needles or pins
- sticky tack
- skewer
- bead with groove for pulley
- string
- two water bottles
- cardboard box
- dominoes
- small drum stick or similar
- several small books
- card
- sticky tape
- a large marble

To design and build the machine, you'll also need tools and supplies, such as:

- pencil and paper
- strong packing tape or sticky tape
- scissors
- glue

Step 1.
First, like Rube Goldberg himself, you need to plan out your ideas on paper, as this makes it much easier to build your machine. Start by picking the task you want to achieve, such as ringing a bell or popping a balloon.

Step 2.
Now work backwards from your task, planning a series of actions. Each action must be triggered by the one before. For example:

TASK: POP A BALLOON

- To pop the balloon, a toy car with a needle taped to the front rolls down a slope and hits the balloon.

- To push the car down the slope, a weight falls into a cup, which pulls up a lever under the car.

- To push the weight into the cup, a row of dominoes is knocked over.

- To knock the dominoes over, the first one is hit by a stick.

- To push the stick over, a line of books falls over onto each other.

- To start the books falling, a ball rolls down a slope.

3.

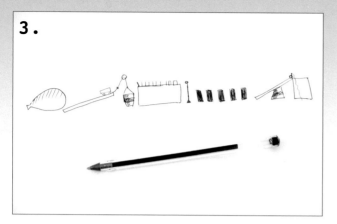

Step 3.

It may also help to draw a sketch of your machine, with arrows and labels to show how it will all work. You can then use this as a guide while building.

4.

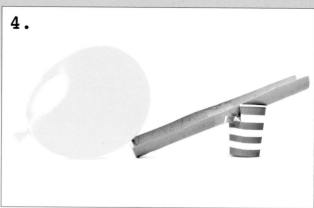

Step 4.

A good way to make a slope is to cut open a cardboard tube, and prop it up at an angle on a paper cup with a slot cut out of it.

5.

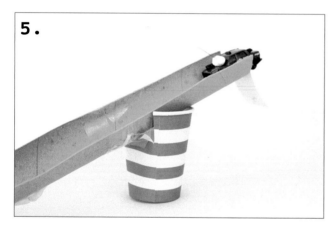

Step 5.

Stick a ball of sticky tack onto the car and stick a needle into it, pointed end outwards, to make a balloon-popper.

6.

Step 6

Make a pulley with a bead on a skewer, suspended between two bottles of water. Loop some string over the bead. Tie one end to the cup and the other end to a paper tab, which fits under the car.

7.

Step 7.

A row of dominoes can be positioned on top of a box, so that when they topple over, the last one will fall into the cup.

8.

Step 8.

Stand a drum stick on the ground where it will knock over the first domino. Secure it with sticky tack.

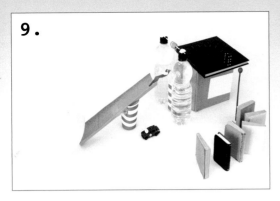

9.

Step 9.
Line up a row of small books behind the drum stick.

Step 10.
Set up another slope with a large marble at the top of it, ready to roll down. Use a piece of paper to block it, ready to be pulled away.

10.

USE YOUR IMAGINATION!

Of course, this is just one example of how a homemade Rube Goldberg machine might work. You can invent your own devices and methods, and make the sequence as short or as long as you like.

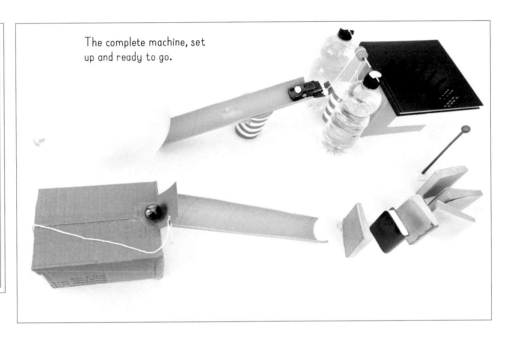

The complete machine, set up and ready to go.

FORCES AT WORK

A good Rube Goldberg machine makes use of as many different forces and movements as possible – like gravity, momentum, pendulum swings, magnets, friction, balance, air pressure and acceleration. Forces are pushes and pulls, and a Rube Goldberg machine is really a sequence of different kinds of pushes and pulls that transfer movement from one end to the other. The other projects in this book might give you even more ideas for things to include.

This example of a Rube Goldberg machine uses weights, a pulley system and a spring to blow up a balloon.

GLOSSARY

accelerate To increase in speed.

air pressure A force exerted on something by the weight of air, or by compressed air.

air resistance A force that slows down an object as it moves through air.

amphibious Able to travel through both air and water.

applied force A force that acts in direct contact with an object.

compress To squeeze, press or make smaller.

conservation of momentum A law of physics describing how momentum can pass from one object into another, instead of disappearing.

density The amount of matter a substance or object contains compared to its volume.

detergent A type of cleaning substance, such as washing-up liquid, which works by separating grease and dirt from surfaces.

drag A force that slows down an object as it moves through a liquid or gas. Air resistance is a type of drag.

electric force A pushing or pulling force between objects that are electrically charged.

energy The ability to do work or make things happen.

force A push or pull that makes things move, stop, change direction or change shape.

friction A force that grips things or slows things down when their surfaces press or rub against each other.

gravity A force that pulls objects towards each other. The larger the object, the greater its force of gravity.

kinetic Something that is caused by movement.

molecules Tiny units, made up of connected atoms, that substances are made from.

momentum The tendency of a moving object to keep moving in the same direction.

motion Another word for movement.

pendulum A weight hanging from a fixed point and able to swing freely.

surface tension A pulling force between the molecules in a liquid, which makes the liquid behave as if it has a 'skin' on its surface.

upthrust An upward force exerted by a liquid or gas on an object that is floating in it.

FURTHER INFORMATION

WEBSITES ABOUT FORCES

Physics4Kids
www.physics4kids.com/index.html

NASA Space place: What is gravity?
spaceplace.nasa.gov/what-is-gravity/en

Explain That Stuff! Forces and Motion
www.explainthatstuff.com/motion.html

Science Trek: Forces and Motion Facts
idahoptv.org/sciencetrek/topics/
force_and_motion/facts.cfm

WEBSITES ABOUT MAKING

Tate Kids: Make
www.tate.org.uk/kids/make

PBS Design Squad Global
pbskids.org/designsquad

Instructables
www.instructables.com

Make:
makezine.com

WHERE TO BUY MATERIALS

Maplin
For electronic components and making projects
www.maplin.co.uk

Hobbycraft
For art and craft materials
www.hobbycraft.co.uk

B&Q
For pipes, tubing, wood, glue and other hardware
www.diy.com

Fred Aldous
For art and craft materials and books
www.fredaldous.co.uk

BOOKS

Fantastic Experiments with Forces (Mind-Blowing Science Experiments) by Thomas Canavan and Adam Linley (Gareth Stevens Publishing, 2017)

Fearsome Forces (Strange Science and Explosive Experiments) by Mike Clark (The Secret Book Company, 2017)

Home Lab by Robert Winston and Jack Challoner (Dorling Kindersley, 2016)

Science in a Flash: Forces by Georgia Amson-Bradshaw (Franklin Watts, 2017)

Science in Infographics: Forces by Jon Richards (Wayland, 2017)

PLACES TO VISIT

National Science and Media Museum, Bradford, UK
www.scienceandmediamuseum.org.uk

Science Museum, London, UK
www.sciencemuseum.org.uk

Museum of Science and Industry, Manchester, UK
msimanchester.org.uk

Smithsonian National Air and Space Museum, Washington DC, USA
airandspace.si.edu

INDEX

DISCOVER MORE...

SCIENCEMAKERS

978 1 5263 0546 6

Understanding sound
Found sounds
Talk to the tube
It came from outer space!
AKB48 bottle train
Turn it up!
Underwater ear
Seeing sounds
Get into the groove
Sonic sculpture
Intruder alert!

978 1 5263 0542 8

Understanding forces
Speeding car stunt ramp
Newton's cradle
Making flight history
Pressure diver
Rocket power
Floating on air
Whale race
Pendulum art
Kinetic creations
Follow the force!

978 1 5263 0544 2

Understanding living things
Miniature plant world
Fast flowers
Colours of nature
Close-up creepy crawlies
Animal movement
Weave a web
Hear your heart
Body copy
Building blocks of life
Fabulous fossils

978 1 5263 0526 8

Understanding light
Art in shadows
A new view
Curved light
A closer look
Make the world upside-down
Sun prints
Painting with light
Garden gnomon
Lightbox display
Neon sign

978 1 5263 0550 3

Understanding machines
Thing flinger
Cable delivery!
Powered flight
Weather machine
Bubbles galore!
At the touch of a toe
Snack machine
Flapping bird
Vibrobot
Robot tentacle

978 1 5263 0548 0

Understanding states of matter
Chocolate art
Summer slushies
Crayon creations
Instant ice cream
Glue gun art
Melting ice people
Desert cooler
Save your life at sea
Evaporation art
Recycled paper

WAYLAND
www.waylandbooks.co.uk